After God's Own Heart

Vbook Collection:

Intimacy With God

Lauren Valler

CONTENTS

ACKNOWLEDGMENTS

I would like to express my gratitude and give glory to God for leading me to write this book for whoever encounters it, may it truly bless you. I am forever grateful to my wise Nanny Betty who advised prudently on the content and added some incredible ideas throughout the chapters. I have been gifted with Graham Healing throughout my author journey with his proof reading and heart towards Vbook and this endeavor to reach hearts and souls. Aimee Stanley for her passion to see this ministry flourish. Thank you, Renewal, for your wise, sound scriptural teaching. I am forever thankful to my family, friends and all my loved ones.

1 THE BEGINNING

We all accumulate so much knowledge and information over the years we almost forget that God is Spirit. It's good to seek and search, but this book will only serve its purpose if we seek the voice of the one who truly speaks. I understand that some of you might not yet know God and desire to start a new relationship, or perhaps you do and are seeking a more intimate connection with your higher power. I believe we are led to books to speak to us in certain seasons, so my prayer to God is that we do not let this become just another book that gathers dust on our bookshelf or Kindle, but that we all use it as a tool to help develop our relationship with Almighty God and then pass it on to loved ones too. What does chasing after God's own heart actually mean? To chase after something is recognized as following, pursuing, seeking after with determination. Spoiler alert, maybe it's not about chasing God's heart as if He's some distant being we ought to run after, quite possibly it's about inviting Him into ours, in order to know and serve Him better.

This book may refer to God by different names throughout, but that's the beautiful thing about an all present, omniscient, infinitely divine force that lives within His believers. I am very clear that I have the upmost respect to all associations to the one true living God, whoever that is to you, however you see and interpret this phenomenon, presence and profound Lord. My heart's desire is that we all re-connect to the heart of Almighty, that as we draw near to Him, He will draw near to us, beautifully awakening us all to our purpose as His beloved children.

The foundations for the wisdom shared in this book may resonate to those who have studied scripture, but I must emphasize that wisdom comes from God Himself. Therefore, always be praying that His Spirit speaks to you personally as you journey through these inspired words. I have no intention to take away or add to any truths of God's word but have every intention to believe that His Spirit can ignite this book to impact every reader who encounters it, as it has done mine.

The beginning chapter is the starting point of sixteen thought provoking areas that can be applied to your relationship with God, that will enhance it significantly, if you put the effort in. There are specifically sixteen chapters to represent the intention, basis and true anointing over this book, **love.** There are sixteen qualities of the love that God desires for us to embody. Love is patient, love is kind, it does not envy, it does not boast, it is not proud. It does not dishonor others, it is not self-seeking, it is not easily angered, it keeps no record of wrongs. Love does not delight in evil but rejoices with the truth. It always protects, always trusts, always hopes, always perseveres. Love never fails. Love is God. God is Love.

We know that love is the answer, yet have you ever felt that something was missing in your life even when you have loved ones so close? Almost an empty void that nothing can satisfy or fill? We all have that hole, and truthfully, we all have those lows. That's because we try to fill it with momentary pleasures, a new home, car, job, partner, and things of the world. But what happens when we've got all of those things? These things can satisfy us for a moment, but God completes us for a lifetime, His love lasts forever. It's a God shaped hole that only He can fulfil. It's no coincidence that you have chosen this book, it's a God-incidence and He's preparing your heart for all He wants to reveal to you through this precious time together.

God, *Supreme Being.*

2 INTENTIONAL

We all have choices in life, and the way in which we spend our time will determine the outcome of our hearts condition. What we listen to, see and hear influence us in ways that are sometimes out of our control. But we can become more aware and purposeful, becoming more intentional with our time. Disciplining ourselves to focus on the things that are lovely, pure and true, then our heart will assuredly overflow with things such as these too. Congratulations, you have now made an intentional decision to focus your mind on the beautiful words in this book, I pray they feed your heart, soul and spirit as you grow in intimacy with your Heavenly Father. May anyone who encounters this book become aware of His saturating loving presence around and within you as you devote your time into seeking His heart. I am so grateful you are here, and I earnestly pray to God that you know of the unconditional, passionate, infinite love that He has for you. Please rest and let Him do a powerful work within you.

Almighty God is seeking to know us all personally, we've all got to find our own spiritual connection to His great power, and we will all experience such unique and different ways of enlightenment. This process can take time; however, God loves us exactly as we are, His grace is more than sufficient. Let's go all in on this relationship, what have we got to lose? If we don't try, we'll never know.

If we love God, we are sharing a message we believe in. Our callings may differ, but God's heart remains the same forever. Some of us will be sent to preach, others to serve, He'll strategically choose some in business and sports, others in ministry, some will teach or write. Some of us will be encouragers, healers, evangelists, teachers or leaders.

It's not always about what we do for God, as we may already be exactly in the ministry that He intends for us, but it's about who we are. He can work through spiritual and earthly gifts, talents, pain, even dire circumstances and weaknesses, anything that will ultimately bring Him the glory. If you've been brave enough to pick this book up, you have a God given calling. He wants to use you as an instrument for His glory, healing and miraculous power that will work through you to leave a message to the world. We serve a generational God, there is no time to a transcendent being, so there has never been a better time to invest in getting our hearts and minds open and prepared for Him working powerfully through us. Let's be intentional with making sure we don't limit God, when He is able to do exceedingly and abundantly more than we could ever ask or think!

Perhaps it's time for us all to re-evaluate any expectations, dreams or visions we may have thought were from heaven and to truly make room for God to speak His hearts desires into our hearts. In our humility Almighty shows His favour, in our weakness He is strong, when we earnestly seek, He is found.

Of all of the self-help books available today, of all the visualization techniques and positive affirmation materials on the market, you were led to choosing this exact book. If you truly want what God wants, this was written specifically for you. However, if your intention is to fit God into *'your plans'* then the humble nature of this book may challenge you, but please have patience. God fits us into *'His plans'*, He has a plan for our lives. God appoints people for things close to His heart and His vision for our lives has a set time, so we're exactly where we are meant to be right now. Everything that we have been through prepares and equips us for the next level and when looking back we can have the wisdom to see God's hand in all of our circumstances all along.

I pray to God that every struggle and limitation is broken off you now as you prepare yourself to hear expectantly from God, the whisper within or the divine thoughts that you become aware of by gently seeking Him in this moment. His desire is that we become fruitful, that we overflow with gifts and power from within to reach the world around us. Victory to victory, glory to glory. Intentional living is being purposeful, contributing to the world, surrendering to something greater than us. We can spend time reading, worshipping, being present with loved ones - but are we intentional? Are we fully engaged in the present moment, and worshipping in Spirit and truth from the depths of our soul? It's time to be intentional with our passionate pursuit for God.

Elohim, *Mighty one*

3 TRUSTING

For some, trusting doesn't come easily, as people by nature let us down. Nevertheless, the ability to trust can be learned and developed. The best place we can enhance this skill is humbly trusting in the one who is most faithful. If you've made a decision to serve God, He requires trust beyond our understanding, beyond logic, it's the way He develops our faith in Him. Yes, it's absolutely necessary to love people, but if you're serious about chasing God's heart, He will give us all the revelation in our own time that putting Him first, trusting Him above all else will take us places that we could never get to by our own logic or strength. Our world view is formed through what we've experienced in our environments, parents, up-bringing, school and everything we've been taught throughout life. The things of the world, also described as the treasures that don't last, will always be based on conditions. Whereas God is eternal, freely offering pure unconditional love that lasts forever.

Have you ever wondered how you've become the person you are today? Do you like who you are? How can we all become the people we really want to be? The purpose of this book is to find your true self in God and how He sees you.

We're so loved, favoured and protected that we simply cannot go wrong, we just learn and grow closer to God with every season that we trust Him in. If we trust in the Lord and ask for His wisdom that He gifts us with generously, this makes His heart glad and enables us to courageously chase after the treasures of His heart.

Trust is described as having a confident expectation, a hope, loyalty, to believe in the honesty, integrity, justice of something or someone. It's being obedient in believing God's faithfulness regardless of what our current situation might look like, as a believer we have been promised that all things work together for our good. Trust works both ways, if Almighty can trust you with the little things, be very prepared for the next level of favour. Let's make every effort to keep our hearts pure, remember that God looks into our hearts whilst people look at the outward appearance. If our intentions are pure, trust that God will honor our hearts desires. Keep focusing on Him, delighting in Him and He will grant them.

We should make every effort to renew our minds, as that is where the battle is. If we don't fill it with the good stuff it will allow room for anxiety, fear and doubt. Allow the Holy Spirit to renew thinking patterns, we can become more aware of our thoughts by taking every thought captive and making it obedient to what God says in His word. Those who truly trust in God, although we will sometimes waver in our faith or thinking, we can wholeheartedly trust in Him and His promises. We all have choices, we all hear voices, yet we can make a decision today to choose to trust and discern God's voice above all.

God is Spirit and the way He will communicate to us to lead us will be so personal and profoundly beautiful. A gentle whisper, a thought, a stirring, a prompting, so intimate for each believer. When at times we may be unsure of what to do, we can lean into Almighty God and enter into His presence, He will gift us with peace and guidance. We only see things and people at face value, remember that the Lord examines hearts, minds and motives so He will forever know what and who is best for us. In a noisy world, we ought to pray to hear our Heavenly Father as He will never let us down. He may have to shake us to move us into where He is leading, to prevent us from doing our will and not His, but His will is always better.

It is a safer route planned strategically for us, secure and without harm, full of fruits and prosperity.

You'll look back in years to come and think, wow God's hand was in my assignment all along. The more we can die to our ego, flesh and people pleasing ways, the more on fire for God we are able to become. It's time to choose calling over comfort. Trust that every situation that we find ourself in is all a part of His plan. Although we may feel uncomfortable at the time, trust that the pieces will eventually fit together, and it will always be turned into good.

When something didn't quite work out, or we face an unexpected obstacle, that will be God protecting us from something we couldn't quite see at the time, we only piece things together when we look back. Let's open our ears to hear His voice and make it our mission to follow His infinitely wise leadership. He wants us to go from victory to victory, where everything we put our hand to will prosper. If we are strong and courageous, the favour of God will be upon our life exceedingly abundantly more than we could imagine.

If we're serious about His will being done in our life, then it takes tremendous trust in God leading us into the unknown. It's time to get excited about all that God has in store for us! If we truly believe, we can ask Him to prepare our hearts for the impossible to be made possible with Jesus. If we ask anything according to His will, He hears us!

If we have a seed of a miracle, a stirring, a passion, a vision, a dream and we've sought God's heart to know it's truly from Him, then simply – **Go For It.**

El Shaddai, *Almighty.*

4 RELATIONSHIP

In order to know where we are going, we ought to know who we are following. Time and time again I hear prayers from people asking God for His purpose for their lives, me included. Yet the penny dropped when I had the revelation that as long as we have the child-like faith to trust our good shepherd each day, He will always lead us the wisest way. That's what trust and faith is, not seeing the whole picture or necessarily having the masterplan, but wholeheartedly trusting that God will lead the way. Let's cultivate an intimate relationship with our Leader, knowing Him, learning from Him and imitating Him will help His plans and purposes unfold for us. I know we all want the answers right now, yet the best thing we can experience is the mysterious.

Wise mentors have advised that we can't possibly see the plan unfold by looking forwards, it's only when we glance back that we see the supreme hand of God working things together for our good. We should all examine our hearts to make sure we don't become too religious on our walk with

Jesus, as this will stifle the freedom of the Holy Spirit working powerfully within, taking us all on a wonderful adventure. We are set free, not bound by the laws of religion but we are reconciled to God through a relationship with His one and only son, Jesus Christ.

We are unique, gifted and will all have a distinctive contribution to make to the world, a legacy to leave orchestrated by God Himself. The more we seek Him, the more of Himself He will reveal to us. Almighty has the most beautiful story written specifically for us, and all He seeks is a humble surrendered heart. Now would be an incredible time for us all to re-evaluate our relationship with God, as we search the depths of ourselves to nurture our connection with Him and grow into all that we are called to be. Our potential is limitless.

These simple probing questions are designed to help us all grow in God, please ensure that we do not feel any condemnation whilst reflecting, as we will naturally desire to want to do these things as our relationship blossoms abundantly over time.

Do we listen as much as we pray? Do we pray according to His will or ours? Do we study as much as we request? Do we suggest or surrender? These simple questions, which in honesty convict the most devoted of believers will help us to create a fruitful relationship with Jehovah. What does a relationship need to flourish? Quality time, honest vulnerability and communication. If you have a heart's desire to grow closer to God that is incredible, and I earnestly pray to God that these words speak to your heart as your Heavenly Father woos you even closer to Him.

Worship, Word and Walk. We can build our faith by spending time seeking His face, pouring out our hearts and souls to Him through intimate simple prayer, worshiping in spirit and truth, reading His word, being encouraged through other believers and books like these. So, let's allow the Holy Spirit to flood through every part of us, every hurt, disappointment and broken part so that God's love can flood through us. Let love heal, be vulnerable and honest with God as there is nothing that we can hide from Him. A relationship flourishes from dedicating focused time in His word, earnestly seeking His Spirit of wisdom and revelation that teaches us all things. Taking time to be outdoors in nature draws us even closer to the all-wise Creator, who has gifted us with the beautiful priceless scenery that surrounds us, walking and talking with Him as one would do with a friend will help us grow in true intimacy.

God requires a child-like faith in our relationship with Him, to lean less on our own knowledge and dive into the depths of His wisdom and guidance. Becoming best friends with Jesus makes us invincible to this world, if we put on the full armor of God, we will be able to withstand any schemes of the enemy. If God is for us, who can possibly be against us?

When we are in a relationship with God, He calls us to be relational with all people around us regardless of their background. Wisdom teaches us that we need to relate to others in order to reach them where they are and where they are at in life. No one is unworthy of God's love. Once we build a relationship at this level, we are much more able to make effective disciples, which is God's will for us. If we desire to be powerful and purposeful for the kingdom, we need to imitate Jesus's example who treated everyone with respect and compassion, a humble servant yet with great wisdom and power. A man is no greater than the level of his devotion, and with devotion comes direction. If we truly dedicate ourselves to the Lord, His direction will follow.

Many claim to believe in God, yet a wholehearted commitment to follow Him is a different thing all together. Religion will only tell you what you ought to do, a relationship will guide you intimately in how, when and where to do it. Please choose relationship over religion, we are called to live in the freedom of the Holy Spirit always, it's time to take off any religious burdens that weigh us down from following God's heart.

Creator, *all-seeing*.

5 LISTENING

Faith is believing without seeing. It's trusting without fully knowing. It's risking without fear of the future or failure of the past. When we trust in God, how can we fail? Each season, trial and test give us an opportunity to grow closer to Him and to refine our character. If we knew we couldn't fail, what would we do? Perfect love casts out fear so if we seek more of God, who is love Himself, it will enable us to take courageous steps forward to what God has put within our hearts. Some of us may know that dream, or vision that the Holy Spirit has impregnated us with, others like me, are still trying to figure it out! But God loves humility and a total dependence on Him. As our relationship grows with God, we hear His voice and if we keep listening and trusting taking it a step at a time, He will lead the way. What does God's voice sound like? To some people, it is actually an audible voice, to others it's a whisper, a thought, intuition. He may speak in a dream, a vision, through a person. It will always align with

His scripture.

The best thing we could ever invest in, is in our relationship with the Creator. One way to grow in intimacy with the one who loves us most is entering into His presence; it is available everywhere all the time and truly lives within us if we earnestly seek Him. Another layer to add to this devoted time in His presence would be to be more intentional whilst abiding in Him and seeking Him earnestly for the spiritual gifts. The gifts of God are wisdom, a message of knowledge, faith, discernment, tongues, interpretation of tongues, prophecy, healing and miraculous powers. He generously gives us these gifts, distributing them as He pleases, to build His people up. We are all gifted and every good thing is a gift from God.

Growing in intimacy with God will take us to new levels in hearing His voice and guidance. If a disciple is serious about going all in for God it is the continual, progressive steps coupled with the faith-based risks that will take us on the most beautiful adventure of true faith.

Children of God, when we feel something in our spirit, we should listen to that as we live by faith not feelings and having a sensitivity to God's voice is the best skill we can develop. That stirring, that warning, that fire burning, that prompting, these are all ways in which the Holy Spirit will guide us on the path of wisdom. Discernment gives us the ability to see beyond the natural, it's awakening us to the caring guidance of divinity by listening and aligning it with God's word. What is God saying to you today, can you hear Him?

When we follow a leader in any sense we listen to their instruction, we trust them and follow obediently. Jesus was one of the most influential leaders of all and we are now gifted with His indwelling presence to lead us personally and collectively in our communities through His Spirit. Therefore, it is necessary to listen and practice heeding His voice as He takes us step by step in our God given assignments and callings. God will not give us too much that we can't handle the assignment handed to us in one go, but He will be preparing us all through divine timing, positioning and character building within us to complete the task at hand.

Having wise mentors around us to listen to their advice will serve us very well, in a multitude of counsellors our plans will succeed but be careful who plants seeds into us on this journey, and ensure they have good scriptural teaching. Laying the right foundations is absolutely necessary if you intend to be a kingdom visionary, our hearts desire should be to leave a legacy for future generations and also to build something that is sustainable through life's storms, God will reward that.

After completing this book, to add some practical ways to accelerate our God given assignment we could begin by seeking and listening to God for vision and direction. For those who are like me who aren't strategically gifted, seek out and pray for the right people to enter into your life to enable you to create spirit led strategies and grow into all that God has planned for you. Listen to ideas, different views, but always take this back to prayer and God's word, always putting Him first.

When you move, He moves and that's why it is essential to discern His voice first in order to make the best moves. Although Almighty is sovereign and His plans will always prevail, our relationship at times can be seen as a partnership. He has us in the palm of His hand but requires us to walk by faith step by step to wherever He is leading us even when it looks as if there is no way, God will always make a way. As we courageously take steps forward following His leading and guidance, He will favour those plans, all in His perfect timing.

El Roi, *The God Who Sees.*

6 WAITING

Chasing God's heart is more than pushing towards His plans and purposes, it's just as much about waiting on God. There is wisdom in the waiting, something to be learned, developed, refined in our character before entering into our next season. Waiting isn't easy when living in an on-demand culture, and everything is instant and immediate. How can our patience possibly be developed? Yet God's promises manifest when we are patiently enduring, hopeful and believe His word to be true.

Chasing God's heart is also learning about His character, His ways, His infinite mind and divine nature, it is so much wiser than ours. The more we know and seek Him, the more we can walk and talk like Him. In the waiting season these are pivotal moments to abide in God like never before, He will be equipping us, teaching us unfathomable things whilst we lean on Him in expectant assurance that He will do as He promises.

There is much power in waiting and trusting, it's giving Almighty the platform He needs to shine His glory, to show the world His miraculous power and sovereignty. Waiting requires humility, patience and an inner knowing that ultimately God is in control. I know we probably want to make our requests known to Him by running to the throne of grace with courage and boldness to pray for certain things. But wisdom teaches us to make our requests known, then leave them in His infinitely wise hands to trust that He knows best regardless of the outcome and will take care of the rest.

In His divine wisdom we can rest in the knowledge that everything will work out according to His plans, in other words 'everything happens for a reason'. He cares so intimately and personally for us that He will always do what is best. God is with us in the waiting doing a powerful work within us, whilst working in our favour to have us equipped and ready for what He has been preparing us for. It's a time to be excited, to serve a good God that is ready to release abundant gifts, prosperity and divine favour our way.

A true believer understands that sometimes God's plan comes with trials, pain and endurance whilst waiting on our deliverer to rescue us. I understand that in these seasons we can feel hopeless at times, I've been there. But we must never, ever forget that He will never leave us nor forsake us but He will strengthen and uphold us. Waiting on God is a powerful thing, if we are anchored in Him, He will shape our future. So we must keep an attitude of gratitude, a God-like mindset and an agility in our walk of faith to let God lead the way and shape us into the men and women He has chosen. We must stay hopeful and positively expectant that something good always comes from waiting, think of birthdays or seasonal events. We typically wait excited to be reunited with loved ones and receive gifts with gratitude, let's try to enhance our mindsets to think like this in a season of waiting, that God is preparing everything ready for the perfect moment to release that gift, bring restoration, reconciliation, breakthrough or whatever it might be that we're seeking Him for.

Some say that the best things take time, and that's somewhat true as our consecration to God is one of endurance, but we must always keep hope in our heart that we serve a Lord who grants us unmerited favour. Whilst some things, with realistic expectations, may take many years to become fruitful or unfold, other promises and plans may result in Almighty God unexpectantly stepping in with such power that we are thrusted years ahead. Accelerated plans, businesses, ministries and new levels, whatever He chooses to do in our lives. That is why it is extremely vital to stay expectant and be best prepared. When preparation meets with opportunity in those divine appointed times we will see the explosive goodness of God. Even if we don't 'feel' ready, let's move with faith and still take those risks, saying yes to opportunities! We can rest in the knowledge that God doesn't always call the prepared, He prepares the called. He will equip us, so we can remain humble and dependant on Him.

We are His, God's masterpiece, child and instrument to do glorious things in this world but at times this does require waiting on Him. Whilst the plans unfold, during the pruning, the refining stage keep believing that at any moment God can step in and shift everything. We serve a God who is way beyond our understanding so please don't limit His power, if He's asking us to wait, it's for a very good reason. Our Heavenly Father cares so much for all areas of our lives, whilst waiting on one area for provision or breakthrough seek Him in another! It's time to allow the Holy Spirit to enhance every part of our lives, so that we may experience the fullness of God and the strength of His joy.

Immanuel, *God with us.*

7 OBEYING

It's one thing seeking God, yet how do we know what to seek Him for in order to chase after His heart's desires for us? We simply pray according to His will. Have you ever noticed God tends to delay on certain requests, yet others have accelerated answers ready to be released upon humbly asking? That's because His timing is different to ours, it's a part of His plan, when the appointed time is ready, He will release the next gift, or open the right door. At this point our heart is most likely ready, we're better prepared and fully equipped.

It is promised that with obedience come rewards so get ready to receive and never weary in doing good, at the perfect time we will reap what we have sown. If we earnestly seek, surrender and then trust in His plan we will have a peace and joy that is unexplainable, nothing will be too hard for the Lord, so receive His grace and rest. We will have a boundless amount of energy to accomplish the task at hand, our strength will come from the keeper of our hearts. It's time to get excited for the mission that God has entrusted to us and lean on His infinite wisdom and love to guide us to our destiny, walk in obedience with Him and He promises to bless everything we put our hand to.

When we truly love Almighty, we will try to keep His commands and obey that He knows what and who is best for us, as we mature in Him. The most beautiful revelation that we can have is that in order to truly live for Him, we must die to ourselves. A wise lady once explained this by relating it to our egos, the part of us we must first become more aware of, fueling it less in order to have more of His Spirit as we walk in that freedom. She explained it as having a bin of rubbish, full of all the things that we need to get rid of, old habits, past pains, disappointments. Once we have gone through that process, we must refill ourselves with God's unconditional love, His word, and to find out who we truly are in Him.

Boundaries are wise, discipline leads to freedom, we are already set free so let's live like it! Almighty God does not ask us to obey Him without first giving us free will, He has given us guidelines to prevent us from hurting ourselves, but also allows us to make our own choices, gracefully loving us all the same. Surrender truly is the key to obedience, it is the Spirit within us that enables us to live a godly lifestyle.

The Creator of the universe is all-seeing, and in a moment of obedience we might not receive the instant gratification that we desire, but these seeds of faithfulness have not gone un-noticed by our Heavenly Father. In His perfect timing, we can expect to receive the overflow of His favour upon our lives. Obedience equals blessings. Keep doing good, there will be many rewards and hidden gifts God has prepared to release to us at divine appointed times. So, expect the unexpected. A life that pleases God behind the scenes is of so much value to Him. The men or women we are when no one is watching determines the purity of our hearts and quality of our relationship with Him. God absolutely, indefinitely loves us. Therefore, if we love Him too, we'll honour Him.

Yahweh, *I AM*.

8 LOVING

We love, because He first loved us. We forgive, because He forgave us. God sent His son to the world to be the ultimate reflection of His divine nature, to embody the true meaning of love. He paid the price for us because He loves us so much. God is love, so to pursue and chase after the things close to His heart, we ought to do everything in love. It's absolutely necessary to love one another, as He loves us unconditionally and this love should flow through us as we are His vessel to reach those in need around us. It's fulfilling to serve and refresh others, but it's essential for us to be refreshed by the source of love in order to be most impactful for the kingdom. When we truly abide in Him the fruits of the spirit overflow into the lives of others, love, joy, peace, forbearance, goodness, gentleness, kindness and faithfulness. When our relationship is right with God, we become even more relatable to the lives of those around us. We tend to be closest to others, when we are closest to God.

If we have the love of the Father within us, accept that our perception of the world we live in will ultimately change.

God doesn't desire for us to chase after the things of the world when we encounter Him. He will change our desires for such things by drawing us closer to His heart, helping us to be in the world, but not of it. We are chosen, set apart and heaven is our home.

The greatest and most beautiful thing we can do as men and women of God, is to love. Let's make it our priority to adore our Creator with all our heart, soul, mind and strength so we can pass this example onto future generations. Prioritize seeking Him first, His kingdom and righteousness and everything else will be added.

Jesus loves us all equally and wants salvation for us all, but I have witnessed the Holy Spirit specifically choosing and anointing those with hurts, pain and a past to take them from broken, to beautiful. The loving nature of these elect people radiate the passion of how Jesus truly saved their life, if this speaks to your heart, then you are extremely useful for the kingdom. God's Spirit shines light into our hearts, helping us to become the light of the world, healed and purposeful for good works. What if the world had to break some of our hearts so that God could heal it to make it His? I feel so called to express the importance of this, that if we truly want to be an instrument for the Lord, it's relationship over religion. It's surrender over superiority. Love covers all wrongs, there is absolutely no condemnation for those who believe in and belong to Jesus Christ.

We as humans will always be limited, this is why we need grace. We are finite, He is infinite, we see in part, He sees the whole picture. When God stretches us, we are never the same, He will allow the darkest parts of our lives to produce the greatest light and love. The valleys give us the opportunity to grow in intimacy with an all-seeing God, the prayers and tears we weep in these seasons are profoundly more purposeful and heartfelt than the prayers of joy on the mountain top. There is power in pain, wisdom in struggles and an incomparable love we develop for Jesus when He holds our hand through those dark times.

Jehovah Rapha, *the Lord who heals you.*

9 TIMING

When seeking God for a plan or purpose for our lives we tend to have requests as long as our arm of all the things we desire to do to bring Him glory. And yes, bringing Him glory is one of our life's purposes, but unless it's where He plants us, we ought to be wise that we don't do it in vain. We don't always have to explain something to the one who knows everything, all of our gifts, strengths and weaknesses, we just have to surrender and trust we will bloom wherever He chooses to plant us.

There is always an anointing, an ease of grace and peace when we are in the perfect will of God and I had a profound revelation of the Hebrew word 'Qarah' as I earnestly sought the Holy Spirit to speak as I wrote this book. Qarah teaches us that God holds time and chance in His hands, and He appoints us to be in the right place at the right time. When things are delayed, believe it is for God's protection. When our vision lingers, believe it will surely come. When right happenings occur know that this is Almighty God causing the right paths to cross through divine positioning, people will go out of their way to be kind to us. Strategic appointments, being in the right place at the right time, making the right connections are all ways that will enable our God given plans to unfold.

Welcome every opportunity, there is something to be learned from everything we encounter and everyone we meet, nothing is wasted. As a child of God, we all have unmerited favour, undeserved grace and the tremendous blessing of Jehovah upon our life. Be prepared for divine encounters, as God is always on time.

I am so blessed and grateful that God led you to pick this book up, you are being prepared and equipped this very moment for Him to do a very powerful work through you. There is something to be learned in every season, a character defect to be refined to look more like Jesus Christ. If we truly abide in Him, He will plant the right hearts desires within us all, supernaturally leading us to our unique callings. If we delight in Him, He will grant us those hearts desires, but let's make every effort to ensure these are from the right motives and that they honor God.

I've been there when promises seem to take forever, petitions and prayers have been made through many tears, the vision is still only in your mind, you've sown and sown and sown. Keep praying for Qarah and walk by faith knowing that God is always on time, it's impossible for Him to be late.

Though you can't see it now, give it time, wisdom will give you much patience. Timing is everything, there is a season and time for everything we will go through in life. In seasons we will experience sorrow, tears, joy and laughter. Life will teach us how to grieve and mourn, as it is sometimes suffering that leads to a breakthrough, embrace it all.

El Shaddai, *all powerful.*

10 GRATITUDE

At the beginning of the book I referred to chasing God as not being an external thing that we experience but being similar to that of an internal one by inviting Him in, gaining closeness and intimacy with the indwelling of His Spirit. We were created to bring glory to God and express our gratitude to Him for who He is and every good and perfect thing He created, including you and I. There has to be an attitude shift, a change of perception to appreciate where God has us now, with hopeful expectancy that He will do exceedingly more than we could pray for in our future. We get strength to help us face any season in life from God's joy, which is a fruit of the spirit He gifts us with.

Gratitude is a magnet for miracles and when God sees that we can be thankful for the seemingly ordinary things He does within our life; He will bless us abundantly with the bigger things.

Although I don't specifically refer to scripture quotations, I hope those that know God's written word see His perfect will revealed throughout these chapters. Some of the most beautiful parts of the Bible were in fact written in the worst of circumstances, proving the power of joy and gratitude regardless of our situation. Paul was a great man of faith who too, set out to chase after God's heart, I am certain He had no intentions to end up in prison in His divine calling. However, the all-consuming saturating presence of Lord Jesus allowed Paul to remain hopeful, joyful and focused on His mission regardless of what He did or didn't have around Him.

Perhaps the focus isn't always on the end goal of achieving some grand vision for the kingdom, it could well be the every ordinary reflections of our Godly character to those around us. God works best through people and positivity is infectious, the influence this has on those around us will inevitably lead to curiosity into how or why we are this way. We all know it is the joy and peace of the Lord. What our minds and hearts are full of will overflow into what we speak out, how we treat others and respond to situations.

Choose gratitude, if we're serious about seeking out God's purposes for our lives then let's make it our mission to get worshipping like never before! We should humble ourselves to make room for God to move powerfully in our lives, we need to be proactive and practical with our praise. We can express it through psalms, worship, journaling, meditating on His promises and our love for Him, we can pray without ceasing and recount all of the wonderful marvelous things God has faithfully done for us. When we enter into His presence, we never leave the same.

Although all of our prayers may not be in accordance to the specific plans that He has for us, as men and women of God we are always being refined in His presence and aligned to His perfect will. We should always keep a level of humility that yes Almighty God may prophetically reveal a vision or dream for our life, but ultimately, we are not in control. Life is unpredictable, things can happen unexpectantly, but God will always do what is best for us if we truly abide in Him, His protection is perfection.

No plan will fail, every purpose of His prevails so earnestly keep expressing gratitude for who God is, the one who never changes and is forever faithful. Be most thankful to the Creator Himself as opposed to things created. Be grateful for wonderful things like nature, weather, family, all that surrounds us. However, be mindful that things come and go and may only be for a season, but the one true living God is forever and has put eternity in our hearts, we should be eternally grateful for that.

Yahweh Shalom, *The Lord Is Peace.*

11 SURRENDERING

Surrender can be the most difficult part in a believer's life, yet the most freeing and that is what makes it absolutely essential to be used effectively by God. With disciplined choices that produce a profound ability to walk in the freedom of the Spirit nothing will be impossible for us, as with God all things are possible. It is truly when we reach the end of ourselves and die to our flesh and ego that the Spirit begins to do a powerful work within and through us. Our ego fools us into thinking it is protecting us and before Jesus Christ this is all we knew, but now we have a more powerful way of living. Humble submission to God will bring unmerited protection from the divine.

Surrender brings anointing, favour and God's hand upon our life that only He can get the glory for. In order to surrender to something or someone it is wise that we ought to know who or what we are surrendering to. The more time we spend with God, read His word and know Him we will learn to trust Him, resulting in a surrendered heart. We are called to live by faith, that's stepping into the unknown trusting God will always make a way. Without faith-based risks, how can we claim to have faith? This book will serve you as an incredible tool to stir up your faith, yet it will prove itself as useless unless we all choose to step out of the boat and put actions behind our beliefs and teachings.

Seeking, serving, listening, leaping they all work hand in hand. Different seasons will require one or the other, or at times all. Let's learn to develop the gift of discernment to hear God's voice in where He is leading us and allow His perfect love to cast out any fear from taking those leaps of faith into the unknown, time to just trust and surrender!

The greatest of us will be a servant, the wisest of us will be humble, the bravest of us will be surrendered. We typically might not put bravery and surrender into the same sentence, but it is extremely noble and brave to lay down one's life for God, it is trusting that His ways are better than ours, His plans are infinitely wiser and that without Him, we can do nothing.

People in the world may have hurt us or broken our trust, but God never does that because He is forever faithful. Surrender brings strength, when we rest in God, we are acknowledging that it is His divine power working through us that helps us accomplish the impossible.

When we sit down, He stands up. When we are weak, He is strong. When we are humble, He shows favour. There's no magic formular of how to win with God, He doesn't need anything from us. A simple surrendered heart is of great worth in God's eyes. When we release control of trying to do things our own way and in our own timing, surrender will bring us gifts we didn't even know we ought to ask for. He is the God of more than, confident trust in His wisdom and timing will lead us to the revelation that everything works out perfectly, just as it is supposed to.

Jehovah Jireh, *Provider.*

12 BELIEVING

Without faith it is impossible to please God. By choosing this book, you already believe that Almighty has a plan for you, an original specific assignment. If we have faith as small as a mustard seed, God will be able to do exceedingly, abundantly more than we could ever ask or think! There is typically an action needed from the believer in order for miracles to manifest. Reviewing wonders in the days of Jesus, Joseph and Moses their miracles were granted after an act of obedience. Sometimes obedience is just a small step forward in order for the flood gates of heaven to open.

Think about it, Moses had to lift up his rod and stretch out his hand in order for the Red Sea to part and the miracle to happen. The blind man had to wash his eyes in order to see again, the paralytic had to be taken up to the roof and dropped down into the house in order for Jesus to heal him. The woman had to touch the tassels of Jesus garment to heal her illness. The priests had to step their feet into the River Jordan so that the people could walk through.

So many miracles, but when we look at them on a deeper level and how they happened, man had to claim it. Belief and expectancy are key, to believe for something we begin preparing for it. An unwavering hope it will manifest as we step forward one step at a time, planning for the vision, walking by faith not sight. Intimacy with God is absolutely essential here, we must yield to Him, abide in Him and seek His heart in order to have the confidence that we are heading in the right direction. God admires fearlessness working hand in hand simultaneously with obedience, He has us in the palm of His hand so we can take courageous steps forward bravely.

When we are in the perfect will of God, there is peace. Have you ever heard someone say if you have peace about a situation or decision after praying that you made the right choice? Well that's the beautiful thing about an adventure chasing God's heart, the path may not always be the easiest, or the one you expected but if Jesus is in it, He will be your peace.

If we ask anything according to God's will, He hears us. If we believe in what we pray for, He will answer. It's not always in the way we expect, but we can't possibly fathom or fully understand God's ways. It's necessary to trust and believe they are much wiser and better than our own. If we delight in the Lord, and selflessly seek out His heart, He will give us our hearts desires. That's not to say we should have a list of all the things we'd like, and God will give them us, but humbling ourselves to truly want what He wants for our lives, for His glory.

Almighty God knows our heart, He knows all of our dreams, visions and hearts desires. Please believe that if they are from Him, those plans will prevail! If your vision is straight from God's heart, He will be equipping you, molding you, preparing you for the next level where your dreams come true. Without belief life would be pretty dull, we'd settle where we are at, accept what is handed to us with no hope for the future.

Yes, it is extremely wise to be grateful and thankful for what we have now, it's wise to rejoice in all things. However, it is belief that gets us through the worst of times, belief that things will get better, belief that a new season is around the corner, belief that God will prove Himself as faithful. We as humans are flawed, if we are humble enough to admit it, we all have weaknesses and insecurities. Yet in our weakness, God's power rests perfectly on us. We must believe that even in those areas, His love and favour can make us whole, complete and able to achieve anything.

What are you believing God for right now? Healing? A miracle? Provision? A breakthrough? As the nature of this book is written in how to become more intimate to the one true living God, let's believe for intimacy that His power can achieve what you are believing for. Truly in your heart believe that as you have dedicated this time focusing on these Holy Spirit inspired words you have drawn even closer to God, and as a result He has drawn even closer to you.

Put Him first, and you will see His hand in all things. There is much impact in accountability, now would be an incredible time to say a personal prayer to God, your higher power, the true source of all. Being respectful of all beliefs will help us to win many people to Jesus Christ. If this is your Lord too, loving all people regardless of their background will help us build many relationships, unaware that we will be influencing people with the precious anointing of the Holy Spirit. Let's invite Him into our hearts like never before, this book almost serves as a third-party, when we all have the infinite access to the heavenly realms right within our reach. Pray, Rest, Believe.

Dear Lord Jesus,

Thank you for dying on the cross for my sin. Please forgive me.

Come into my life. I receive You as my Lord and Saviour.

Now, help me to live for you the rest of this life.

In the name of Jesus, I pray.

Amen.

El Olam, *The Everlasting God.*

13 VISION

Without faith it is impossible to please God. By choosing this book, you already believe that Almighty has a plan for you, an original specific destiny for your assignment. Without vision, of who God is and His perfect will, people perish. Imagination is a beautiful thing, as children we have more freedom to imagine all of the things we hope for in the future, it's an incredible tool for creativity. Yet as we grow older, the pains and troubles of this world stifle our imagination, we become conditioned to our environment and our mindset suffers as a result.

My prayer is that the Spirit of God opens our minds up creatively, to think bigger, better, to be visionaries. You might be reading this in the comfort of your own home, that's wonderful, or commuting, travelling to a destination but here's a challenge, take time to visit somewhere you feel free. Go somewhere that enlightens your creativity, visit a new place, or a place you're fond of! It's time to nurture the inner child, we all have one.

Perhaps we've all at times become a bit rigid, we've followed the rules, Groundhog Day has kicked in and we're stuck in either religious ways or a life we're not fulfilled in. The Greek translation of fulfilment is 'pleroo' which means to fill up, to make full, to fill completely. So if we're seeking vision, it's wise to seek the one who gives it to us! And we can do that by asking God to fill us completely with His Spirit and the visions will follow. God longs to give good gifts to His children, and He promises to gift us with His power generously to all who ask.

If you're interested in focusing specifically on gaining prophetic insight from God for the vision He has for you, I have created some practical workbooks through Vbook that you are able to download immediately for free at www.vbookz.org. If we want to leave our mark on the world that takes true bravery, those that are truly set apart to be used as a powerful instrument for the Lord can gain confidence through His indwelling presence, call it 'Godfidence'. This power within us all will help us to press on towards our goals and callings, with favour and anointing.

If you're blessed enough to have already had a revelation from God and you've truly discerned that the vision is heaven sent then that's incredible! Edification will be a vital next step for you, nurturing the vision, protecting it, building yourself up in the faith and surrounding yourself with the dreamers, the doers and those that will encourage you.

Visions are to be shared, but they are also to be protected. As a child of God we will always face opposition, the greater the calling and responsibility entrusted to us, the greater the sacrifice, discipline and trust in God required.

Do you believe God will do as He's shown you? The voice we choose to listen to will determine the acceleration of the vision. We must not allow doubt, the enemy or people's opinions to enter into our minds or hearts, instead focus on God's voice, His promises and continually build ourselves up in His word and through worship.

Visions can be like seeds, dropped into our hearts and minds from God's divine hand, and it's our responsibility to cultivate them. It's very much the same with an idea, it will only ever stay as an idea unless we manifest it into existence! Vision requires creativity, to see beyond the natural, to believe in the supernatural. God reveals wisdom and mysteries through His divine Spirit, so the closer we are to Him, the more He will reveal to us.

If we make it our mission to follow Him, He will develop our vision, faith and character to do wonderful things that bring Him glory. God may have one very specific vision in mind for us, but He cares so intrinsically for all areas of our lives, so don't box Him in or limit Him! He will have prophecies ready to be revealed for our family, career, ministry, adventures to travel, home, His desire is that we prosper and become fruitful in all things!

It's always great to reflect back on Almighty's faithfulness when hoping for the future, although let's remember that our hope is found in Jesus. Have you ever had a vision before that came true? Recounting God's faithfulness to build faith whilst tapping into His infinite source of creativity will enable you to envision, then prepare and most importantly believe!

El Rachum, *The God of Compassion.*

14 GROWING

A new level requires a newer version of us, a more refined character. By choosing this book you have already made the intentional choice to grow spiritually. Growing in God is the greatest goal, and time spent with Him is never wasted. The knowledge we acquire today will be the wisdom we need for tomorrow. Every investment we make into God's kingdom will bring a harvest if we do not give up, as a man sows, he reaps and if we choose wisely to sow into the kingdom, be prepared for an overflow of favour at the appointed time. It takes discipline to seek God continually as a priority, when we begin to write the word onto our hearts and invest in knowledge and wisdom through books such as these, the revelations will be brought back to memory at the perfect timing when we need it most.

I believe you are a Spirit led believer, well if you've made it to this chapter I will assume and pray you've encountered God in fresh ways on your journey with Vbook, so it is absolutely vital to be continually refreshed by the Spirit of God to gain even closer intimacy with Him. It's through His word and presence that we experience revival and grow deeper in our relationship with Him. God desires to stretch, test, prune and humble us so we can grow into true disciples, a perfect reflection of His divine character.

If we were to look at the back of a cross stitch without seeing the front of the finished picture it might look somewhat messy, yet without that beautiful strategic mess we wouldn't have the final refined picture that God sees, as His masterpiece, because of His Son. We are made in His image and washed clean with His Spirit.

Growth can be painful; change can feel uncomfortable but it's in these moments we reach new levels in our faith. Some say that new levels result in new devils so always be on guard with the full amour of God to withstand the storms and trials of life as we grow in maturity and wisdom.

Some seasons may well be opposition from the enemy, but God will never give us too much that we can't handle life, as everything is under His authority. In these testing times lean and press into Him like never before knowing that it is His strength and peace that will see us through, whilst we wait for His deliverance. We can't necessarily grow when things are all hunky-dory so let's prepare our heart for all aspects of our assignments, the greatest heroes are given the greatest tasks.

God has given us the gift of life, with the indwelling of His Spirit to enable us to grow into all He is calling us to be.

Growth is a process, a refining season and it is good for us to change, to never regret the people we were but to improve the people we are. Humility teaches us that there is always something to be learned, always someone to be served and growth in God is the greatest adventure we can all go on. If the Holy Spirit truly lives within, we simply cannot stay the same. God will bring out gifts, talents and fresh anointings we didn't even know we had.

El Sali, *The God of Strength.*

15 TRANSITIONING

There is a time and a season for everything we will go through in life and it's so easy to miss the present blessings and miracles when we are focusing too much on the past or future. There is always a process of preparation and in a time of transition it is absolutely OK to feel frustrated or impatient, we're human. In a time such as this it's vital to try our best to not react out of the frustrations of our feelings but respond out of the fruits of our faith. The fruits of the Spirit are love, joy, peace, patience, kindness, goodness, faithfulness, gentleness and self-control.

Whilst transitioning from one season to another, or God closing one door in preparation to open another, reflection, refocus and refining are key. Let's try not to lose ourselves in the noise of the world or become too anxious for the things of the future but make it a priority to be in the present moment, trusting the one who holds our future. It's time to release the chains around us that have kept us a prisoner to our past, to transition into a life of true freedom.

We are held in the palm of Almighty God's hand, every hair on our head is numbered, He knows what is best for us all individually and collectively. His perfect will allows us to walk in freedom and His directive Spirit helps us to follow Him trustingly with a beautiful child-like faith.

There is a reason we pray for our daily bread and pick up our cross each day because we can't possibly predict the exact course of our lives, that's God's job and it is wise to trust Him each day, step by step. In a process of transition our faith will be stretched and our trust in God tested as we let go and release the things of the past, to prepare for the fruitful things of the future. If we hold on too tightly to anything in this world how can God possibly release the next gift that He has for us? Release to receive, let go and let God.

Think of a house move, we declutter our possessions and remove the things we have outgrown, saying goodbye to the things of old whilst making room for the things of new. God is bringing us into a spacious place, and in that period of transition we shed the things we wouldn't want to bring into a new fresh clean place. It is the same with our character, certain habits, attitudes and limitations will need to be refined by the Holy Spirit as we level up. The same could be respectfully said for the people around us, some of them just aren't assigned to our next season or level and in that transition phase God will be removing and replacing according to His plans, purposes and preferences. There is always a process of healing from the pains of the past in order to propel into the purposes of the future.

Following God whole heartedly is not always easy! It requires, at times, hurting feelings to move passionately towards our God given mission.

The bravest of us will prioritize God and His leadership over the opinion of others. As we transition beautifully from victory to victory let's allow God's Spirit to do a powerful preparation within us, a refueling and refreshing ready to elevate us to new levels. An open attuned mind is key to allowing God's voice to guide us into new places, provision and prosperity as we obediently follow the Fathers heart.

Let's discipline ourselves to see the transition phase as exciting not exasperating! Allow faith to build up to make room for the God of the impossible to step in at any time and wow us. The God that I serve is an all-loving, good, mighty God and He wouldn't have us waiting if He wasn't preparing something way beyond our comprehension, so trust the transition process and believe for His best. We are all about to understand God's heart on a deeper level than we ever have done before, what we are all reaching for is already ours. We are His, and He is ours.

Yahweh Tsuri, *Lord My Rock.*

16 THE END

With access to an overwhelming amount of information that surrounds and clouds our minds, my prayer to God is that this book has helped you discover your own truth in Him. It's really quite simple, if we don't allow the truth to renew our minds and His Spirit to refresh our souls, we will all wander aimlessly as lost sheep. Just follow and He will lead. Almighty God has chosen and found us, He lives within and His wisdom is generously available to all who earnestly call on Him. He desires to lead us each day, opening and closing the right doors to guide us in His plan that He has for our lives. When one door closes, another opens. When one season ends, another begins. As one method of provision dries up, God leads you to another more fruitful place. Although it may be the end of this book, it's only the beginning of eternity spent with Jesus, who is the same yesterday, today and forever.

In summary, relationship over religion will help us to abide in God's grace, love and strength. We are saved by grace not works and therefore have access to unmerited favour if we believe. Being grateful in the present moment will enable us to enjoy what God has gifted us with whilst He prepares us for the bigger things. Love God, love people. Trust God over people.

Make it a priority to seek God first and His kingdom, and everything else will be added. Try not to be anxious about tomorrow as each day has enough trouble of its own. Do all things as if we were serving God, bringing glory to Him.

At the end of it all, it's a love story between us and God. We will face many hardships, endure many trials for His name's sake but surely that kind of suffering will never be done in vain? We are His beautiful children, refined and molded to look more like the one who created us. We will experience the valleys and the mountain tops, the comfort, the power and love of God, we will experience it all.

That undeniable, all-consuming presence of the Lord that heals every part of us will never, ever escape us. In the heavens or the depths of whatever it is that we face, His hand will guide us, and He will never, ever forsake us.

Become aware that the only people we can truly change is ourselves so invest most effort here, ensuring our hearts are right before Him, it will give us much peace. Although this book was designed specifically for the reader we are called to go and make disciples, so share this message to others, a comforting word to a hurting heart could plant a seed that could change someone's life forever.

All glory goes to God as I have earnestly and deeply sought His Spirit and wise counsel to breathe life into this book, so the next step I advise in our journey would be to dive into the depths of His flawless unchangeable word for ourselves, that remains the same from generation to generation.

I pray whoever has read this book from heaven God reveals more of Himself to you and you know just how loved you are. May His Spirit refresh, refuel and refocus you as He prepares you for the things close to His heart.

Go For It.

Adonai, *Lord, Master.*

God's Heart For Us

∞

Precious child, He loves you so much
God wants to nurture and protect you
with His Spirit's gentle touch
You're after His heart
But He's after yours
Congratulations, you've got it
Time for a round of applause

He knows you so well
Every need, every hurt
No longer in worry shall you dwell
His love for you is burning
Your ways He will always be learning
But His ways are wiser than ours
So keep seeking Him, He is never far

Infinite, endless, and true
Is God's never-ending love for you
He'll woo you and pursue you
Graciously forgiving all that you do
Compassionate and abounding in steadfast love
The truest kind of love, within yet sent from above

ABOUT THE AUTHOR

Lauren Valler is a humble woman after God's own heart.
A born-again Christian with a true passion for God's kingdom.
An entrepreneur, business and ministry founder. She has a
passion and gift for helping others realize and fulfill their God
given potential.
For further ways to connect with Lauren you can download a
free Vbook at www.vbookz.org with code 'Vbook' as a gift to
further strengthen your journey and relationship with God.

REFERENCES

Bible Study Tools - www.biblestudytools.com

God's Names - www.ibelieve.com/faith/10-powerful-names-of-god-and-what-they-mean-for-us-today

Rick Warren - 'God doesn't call the prepared. He prepares the called'

Salvation Prayer – www.crosswalk.com

If this Vbook has impacted & encouraged you, please review us!

Then who can you pass Vbook onto, to bless & encourage too?

Printed in Great Britain
by Amazon